The Thought Sits W

Ruth Beddow

Published by Nine Pens

2022

www.ninepens.co.uk

ISBN: 978-1-7398274-8-9

012

I have tried to tell it in order without any lies. But then again, how is a person to distinguish what really happens from what one thinks is happening?

Margarita Liberaki, *'Three Summers'*

Pipistrelles

First, the home
we barely remember:
lime lathered walls
and offcut carpet
laid hurriedly
by a neighbour;

>
the burglar
who strips the rooms
of every mundane treasure
but leaves your jelly limbs
bald halo skull
to dream behind the bars;

a paddling pool
a fear of wet
the lesson wasps are bad
and pipistrelles – good.

>
Pipistrelles
every night of July
flit between the conifer trees;

bi-bee-bam
every August noon
chimes by your driveway
halts
for soft serve and screwballs

>
then vanishes
in a beat –
choral

as your brummie voice calls
as you chase after it
through honeyed
suburban heat.

When our mad neighbour died

no tears graced the entrance to his house;
no enormous quantity of carnations draped
the unvarnished truth of the door frame
or the chipped red paint on his unpeopled step.

Soon after, a distant cousin opened up the rooms
and said, *take what you like*, leaving little
to be desired in a dusty mound of folk CDs,
a box room rammed with porn parodies.

Luckily, my mother had a habit of cleaning up
after dead people – some glacial form of empathy
for a periphery of souls, and though I had never thought
him lonely, choking his old cat around the road
on a leash, the thirties semi begged to differ.

I clasped my mouth as she filled black bags
with a whole life, mummified. And while that stench
was sheering through the trees, the usual sadists
of suburbia regaled themselves with other tales:
errant badgers, jamborees. Mortal things.

Forest School

While our parents prophesised the millennium
bug, we were busy building houses for bugs
in the coppice by the school. Busy digging
holes with our fingers, for twigs to steady leaves
like rusted canopies. Some of us clawed at the earth
fervently; some of us knew the task was futile.

I was of the ilk that knew our task was futile.
Scarcely out of pre-school, by the millennium
I'd established a wariness of the earth
and the ambiguities of dirt. (I was terrified of bugs.)
And instinct told me they weren't tempted by leaves
to flee the underworld for whatever we were digging.

Alex, Louise, Josh and Jenny had a field day digging
and I didn't have the heart to tell them it was futile.
At lunch, teacher made us recite the names of leaves
like beech, or birch, not adult words like *millennium*,
terrorism or *recession*. Only those of trees and bugs
as if everything to teach could be taught by the earth.

So there I was with my twig and patch of earth
trying to find a more hygienic way of digging –
that didn't involve so much dirt, so many bugs –
though looking around I realised this was futile
and my method could take a whole millennium
to balance the twigs just so, assemble the leaves.

Somewhere in the afternoon I coveted some leaves
I found, stomping across the blanket of earth,
holding hands with a girl who couldn't say *millennium*.
By now we were done with the labour of digging
so walked in rings around the coppice (quite futile)
as rain embellished my waterproofs like falling bugs.

The day evaporated, as days do, with no sign of bugs
though I trudged home with a fistful of leaves
which mother threw a scrap book, now futile,
since neither of us remembers where on earth
we put it, how deep in the loft we'd be digging
to find it again, so many years from the millennium.

At some point I stopped flinching at bugs and the earth.
I tried to learn the names of leaves; I took up digging.
None of it felt so futile, once we survived the millennium.

Consider the subtleness of the sea

after Herman Melville

Consider your old headmaster in the papers,
the booth at Frankie and Benny's where you read
the headlines and couldn't feign surprise.
Just photographs, they said, mainly boys;
five hundred in total and eighty-eight
in the *worst category*. Consider
what the *worst category* means.

Consider the taste of burnt pepperoni
between your braces as you discussed
whose job it was to grade depravity
and consider the judge's verdict:
his partner had left him,
his life was in turmoil,
he began to live in a virtual world.

Recall years three, four, five –
the changing room in this world;
door ajar for 'health and safety' and him
standing there, staring as you stripped down
to floral knickers, pancake chests dripping
after a game of rounders on the hottest day of July.

Consider rehearsing Joseph (the musical comedy)
in the school hall: he would play the lead
and the puniest child, Mrs Pophitar.

Consider how you laughed and laughed
at his penchant for whale music;

his recordings from Vancouver Island –
the humpback song, the orca's whistle,
the snigger of minke.

Consider laughing until it's not funny anymore:
an intelligent man
a man of good character
a man who friends described
as honest, considerate, and kind.

No one ever asked you how it felt.

Tits

Yours were pointy
like dormant volcanoes –
not capable of much but one day
maybe. In PE class, the netball girls
would tease your bashful lack of bra
and when, after months spent dressing
in the loo, you finally revealed the new-
sheathed contents of your powder shirt,
underneath was a cotton string pre-teen
thing that barely made a difference.
Meanwhile, I learned to carry
a roll-on, lavender-scented
maxi pads I didn't
really need
and on the playing field
would giggle as we agreed
the parameters of unfuckable,
the mating-call necessity of a plunge
or a balconette. *Girls can be so vicious.*
This is something we like to tell ourselves
as grown girls, and looking back, forget
to ask why things tilt this way – why
friends forsake old friends, what
boy-shaped silhouette leers
through the strip of glass
in the door and conjures,
like the sorcerer of tits,
every inch of this.

Birmingham Central Library, 1973

They call It progress
like they called it progress then.
The year my mother married,
when my father was building castles
in the mud. Some things are just too brutal

to withstand time, and perhaps that library
was one of them. Its concrete running
like tears in panstick, its plaster swelling
to the shape of shelves, the smell
of barely opened pages.

All I know for sure is this:
the man who thought the whole thing up,
whose buildings made my father
think up buildings, too, was dead
the moment they announced its demolition

and later, a year since I had left the place
for good – a decade after my parents
dismantled our home – the rubble piled high
on Paradise and said, as I stood watching,
there's a grace in being forgotten.

A gigantic kiss rowed toward him

after Tess Gallagher

On the roof of the new Birmingham Library
(a structure most residents called
an architectural catastrophe)
(a structure we admired
for its reckless steamrolling of the past)
the kiss announced itself unhurriedly
like the swarm of a dandelion head –
all asexual and nearly dead.

Another rowed in later that day
at the Custard Factory
beneath a railway arch
then another, bolder
on platform four at Moor Street
and lastly on the train
where we rocked like brazen stalks
into one another's worlds
and swerved aside in time
when you got off at Dorridge
and nothing ever came of it.

Sun, Sea, Sangria

In reality, our destination was halfway inland –
up an inlet swamped by groundsell and graffitied.

Perhaps in colder months it held the look
of the Guadalmedina, but not that August:

eighteen, two star hotel on the east side of town,
flat fanta lemon warming by the bed

as we compared the texture of our nipple hair
in the slant light between the *rejas*, not knowing

what we wanted from a city. On the second day
we took a train to Torremolinos for omlette and chips –

soles sand-scorched, backs coconut-oiled in a charred year
to be British. 2015: Cameron's England falling

down a monkey ladder and us, infants of free movement, gliding
through customs without a sliver of *Español*.

It could have been dick, plain and simple. Dicks
in cargo pants, dicks on fresh-faced boys

who dragged us through the cobbled streets,
dicks balancing free margaritas oh! how we laughed

open mouthed, tongues seared by tequila –
no more! no more! – though more came anyway.

The morning after, we lined up like cabbage patch dolls
beside the pool and had known each other's bodies

so long, there was no shock to the linger of sunscreen
before we travelled different ways.

Multiples of Me

after Mary Jo Bang

Damp and hand-me-down
the room demands an additional heater
but this would breach dorm policy –

as if you needed reminding
you are still a child, standing at the aperture
of a canary yellow hallway, carpet like garra rufa
biting at your soles. There's a frantic quote

about bathroom mirrors scrawled in biro
across the pinboard – as if your predecessor knew,
as if the ghost of you was always written
on these walls. At midnight,

you flood the laundry room and try to reverse
the tsunami with two saucepans and a ladle.
Had worry failed to seed for larger things,
like cancer, or heart disease, this would have been

a true disaster; had you spent less time
with the thought of dying; had dying seemed
a little harder. Here, in the miniature bathroom

where you shit, shower and brush your teeth
in tandem, then stand before the mirror
with squid ink eyes – shaking, smiling,
and barely recognise the face you clean.

Arrival

I

Julie shouts from her second-floor window
I HAVE THE COUNCIL ON SPEED DIAL
IF YOU CAUSE ANY TROUBLE
and this plastic-clad pile becomes home.

II

Julie's German Shepherd howls as I unpack
a five-tog duvet, free the dying wasp. Examine
suspect stains on the curtain hem and run knuckles
over woodchip, hoping it will have its day again.

III

Julie walks her beast in the square of receding grass
outside our house. Three of us sit on the pink
pleather sofa – a throne we call the Rat Hotel.
Nod Julie's way and Julie squints back.
Her front garden consists solely of marigolds
as if they're all her soil sustains.

IV

Julie unbolts her door as I attempt a parcel drop and run.
The dog's mouth foams like spume on a hot beach.
She says the council are all cunts. In our front garden
fag butts prod through gravel like rotting babies' fingers.
I glance at hers, then begin to weed ours with a fish slice.

V

Julie's lover smokes outside as our party guests arrive.
You can smell his soured cologne through the scarcely open
window. Julie sounds happy, adolescent,
like the ring-pull on her dark fruit cider.
She shoots me a wink as they waltz their way inside.

VI

In those days the kitchen was all table and the fruit bowl
all flies. A single striplight flickered against artrex,
dripped a decade of lard onto peeling lino.
At some point, Julie's dog died and we didn't see her
for some time. The odd thud of Iron Maiden
reassured us she was still alive.

VII

When it was time for our moving vans to pull away
Julie resurfaced at her window like an apparition,
which she wasn't. Shouted something I don't remember
about *new tenants, more trouble, they never stay long*
and waved her ceaseless wave goodbye.

Tight

It took three attempts for him to fuck me.
I couldn't believe he kept coming back
to try again on the glider wheel divan,
his hairless dick somehow tanned and glowing
from a life on the Sunshine Coast,
his horizontal bedside manner perplexed
but not impatient at the portcullis
between my legs – asking if I was sure
I wanted it, which I wasn't.

Instead, we'd watch Bob Ross then stumble
separately downstairs next day.
My flatmates would shoot *the look*
and I'd contort my face to say *not really*
and he and I would catch the Northern Line –
opposite sides of the carriage,
silence sliced by tunnel gusts –
him to Tooting, me to Charing Cross
(one stop sooner than I needed)
where I'd hurry along the Strand
with my pants chafing.

Ode to a Reuterweg Bedsit

Es führt zu nichts, he said
as though honesty was his invention –
an old Germanic tendency for foresight.

That day saw the first rain of September,
the first rain of September as it hung
like frogspawn from his golden lick of hair.

My bag was already packed upstairs
in the matchbox room I had thought Neolithic
but which, in time, as with all the walls we love

and leave, had softened all around me.
This moment, this harlequin step and his four
sterile words were only ever meant to be

one part of this – which I do not tell him,
which I need not say.

Questions to a Mound

I want to ask what the tiny spoons mean,
how the Sri Lankan garnets found their home here
and whether Raedwald was a benevolent king.

I want to know which gods I have neglected
to believe in, if they ever walked the ridges
of this estuary or are known to walk here still –

you sailing backwards in between them, waiting
to reanimate with each stray footstep, every pang
of progress on your hollow heap of peppered earth.

Tell me if you meant for me to walk for miles
and never find you? Here between the crooked pines
where something of a keel line slices sleet

then on my knees in an unrelated field,
sky prized for the baptism I never had
like some Saxon jape that hasn't aged well.

Cleaning It

it's like concrete setting   on my shoulders
it could implode   but refuses   i walk past a man
pissing   in the russell square fountain   it doesn't startle
not like the thoughts   thoughts like hemlock
rooting beneath my feet

i try to work out where they seeded –
was it us   in his ford mondeo   parked up
by the river avon   (i'd lost a baby tooth in my sandwich)
or walking   across the golf course   hand in hand

i force an image of fucking my brother
fucking my friend   fucking a dog   check
between my legs   if I can feel it   & when it twitches
hate myself   even more   want to die

that night   i call him   & we talk about other things
like mother's day   gardening   i want to say
i do not want this   but it sounds insane   outside my head

i take the thoughts on holiday   (vienna)   they fit nicely
in my hand luggage   but i do not enjoy the belvedere
i do not marvel   at the klimt   it does not feel better
to know   which painters shagged their siblings
i cannot stomach the strudel   i visit freud's apartment
& try to ask him   *what is wrong with me*
he is not at home

back in london   the first therapist asks
well   do you want to fuck your brother   ?
& i ask the room   to swallow me
the second says   *this is not within my remit I'm afraid*

25

& for the third i draw a vicious flower
then a scale on paper   hitler to buddha   gherkins
to duty-free milka   & she says
OCD is not just about clean hands

i am three rungs away from adolf
when the timer rings

Dissecting the Pomegranate

The first incision, the opening of her
is a fuschia bloodshed. Thin juice spurts
to far tiles and stains my white, cotton nightie.

I had thought myself the neurosurgeon
of exotic fruit, but the more I look
at her – ivory membrane carved
into neural pathways – the more I seem
to be looking in the mirror
after a craniotomy; impossible vanity
of folded lobes and pear-shaped cells
so sweet, she could be full
of serotonin and dopamine.

I ask myself if eating her would stop
this fear from eating me? Then squeeze
a few between my teeth to see rubies
and rubies in places you couldn't imagine
like the cerebellar cortex, the innermost part
of the pomegranate's psyche where she receives
her own Chinese whispers, where she decided
it was time to fall from the tree

and before I know it
I am crunching her inside out
contorting her skull into backbends
as she divulges, scatters
fresh seed across the counter

and I can't help but ask
if she'd do the same to me –
given the chance –
whether I would gladly let her.

Do you want a chaperone?

I think of the pre-fab stairs,
the acnied boy – his hand
tattooed in biro at the vertex
of my thighs, sliding between
hot tights and loitering like a slug
on my mother's carpet.

No, I think I'm fine.

The doctor's blue latex hands advance
across the examination table –
squeeze a nipple, pummel the armpit,
eyes averted as his fingers read
the hieroglyphs of skin.

*You have naturally
lumpy breasts.*

Thank you.

He doesn't smile.
Tells me to dress up
as though I've wasted
precious time.

Take as long as you like.

Does it hurt?

You were lying when you said it wouldn't.
The measles vaccine, the own brand tampon,
the sting of dead jellyfish on Dyffryn beach;

leaving that place to come home each summer,
leaving home at the end of that summer and never
coming back. Mainly the time you were in the hospital –

there was a gift for every day of your disappearance
which only made it worse. Now I ask myself
what would hurt the most – a choked reading of this

inadequate poem at your funeral, or the cleaning
of your room when you're barely even gone?
And I plan how I'll roll myself up in your deep-pile rug

doused in your last bottle of Anais Anais
like a pagan ship burial – and wait, and wait
for you to come back and set me alight.

Aquaphobia

What happened to the girl who dreaded swimming lessons,
every Saturday morning at Northfield baths? Had to be coerced
by happy meals and milky bars, shoulders thrust high
above the surface of the kiddy pool, snakefly neck craned
towards the clock's smooth red second hand – the girl
who measured time, weighed resistance
in twenty-five metre lengths?

                                                    Did I drown that girl?
Did she sink down
                    to the slick
                            dreg
                                    bowel
                                            of the deep end
                                                    in pursuit of a rubber ring?

The girl who every August hovered one cold sole above
the rockpool at Nantcol – big toe lowered slow, gnawed
by mozzies and magnified beside the stubbled moss that clung,
despite everything. Despite the coked-up father who fell
                        brittle girl piggy-backed
                                down
            down the face of the Falls last summer,
        limbs battered like old haddock, skulls bludgeoned
    and washed up among the pebbles, where the other campers
                        grilled their meat.

Surely not the girl who lowers whole feet, down the creaking
steps into Hampstead pond – shock black basin, unknowable
depth – preferring not to know what life or death
shares that water, toes sliced farther but tanned this time from
a summer spent searing on the heath.

Then pushing out in writhed gasps, heart stalls
catches itself

keep kicking, says
the girl

all this time you thought you were flailing
you were staying afloat.

The Weekend After

i catch fire
my scorched frame
won't collapse
takes its time
throbs breezeblocks
scales cascade
to ash
past old windows
burnt crusts
i want to sleep
but bodies slump
still hot
on floor thirteen
skin corrodes
on twenty three
waiting
to be dragged from
the wreckage
i am stubborn
like a rotten thumb
ink cap mushroom
a black warning
to the sky

every corner
carries mother's face
as if to say
let me remind you
you escaped
she did not
her phone still rings
does she breathe
awaiting rescue
in the bedroom
i stumble aimless
through the borough
i wear the same
putrid clothes
surfing sofas
til i'm found
a home
on top of the world
she used to say
every morning
at breakfast
before sunrise
bleary eyed

bursts magnolias
and London Pride
while summer solstice
floods the city
like hot milk
gushing
through Holland Park
air stifles
outside the violet house
of someone's rich uncle
mojito in hand
sweet pith of lime
hotpants chafing
up to the balcony
barbeque wafts
across a blue horizon
i've never seen
cloudless
but for a monolith
smoking like the
charcoals turning
as I gape
is that Grenfell?

Asylum Hotel

I think of the fish tank elevator
climbing like an experiment in specks
of mango, fuscia, lapis lazuli, towards
the roof of the Radisson in Berlin;

a scorched sundeck at the Hotel Kraft
nestled two streets behind the Arno –
a place my grandparents found in the sixties
before that river burst its banks.

It must be nice to live in a hotel, I say, not thinking

and Eljona recounts four years of fast food,
longing to cook *tavë kosi,* own a lamp,
hearing languages she can't understand
through the walls, except when she leaves
a few hours each day, hears her language
but is afraid speak – mouth unfastened briefly

closes again. On the high street she passes
an aquatics store, where the flowerhorn cichlids drift
edge to edge. Then ambles by the hot dog stand,
the gay bar, through supermarket doors
and up the travelator to the homeware aisle
where she compares photo frames
she cannot fill; Egyptian cotton towels

on sale
last chance.

Dungeness

The day before the world shut
we drove a car to the nuclear coast.
Wind lodged in our throats, groaned
over pebbles and corrugated roofs
which surely, we agreed, remembered
harsher storms than this.

Train tracks led to nowhere.
The smell of fish wrong side of fresh
hung on mangled nets, on air,
on carpets of biting stonecrop
where I crouched to piss
because the pub was closed.

We couldn't speak for gusts
so we held hands, sunk
and clambered over debris
made tender by years of salt
and promised the place –
one day we would come back.

Afterwards, we'll call it frozen time

but it's more like life   on autopilot   plucking your teeth
every morning   moving forwards   then lying back down
on the ground   /   no longing looks   in the mirror
you make   yourself sick   with the news   as tanks weave
adders through wheat   poised for a city   blazing gold
the morning after   a cancelled stag do   /   this
is my fantasy   my apricot silk   a mermaid touching
heaven   walking barefoot   through a cemetery in August
it's dusk   and the air   falls faintly metallic   like an engine
still ticking   like a leaky filling   like a ring unwilling
after hundreds of miles   on this road

All my friends are leaving town

or having babies.
The thought sits with me
on the flight to Tokyo
chasing one of them across Siberia
in a pixel plane
on a fold-out screen.

There is so much
emptiness beyond the wing
I can almost feel it
in the inch of glass
that promises
to hold us all together.

All my friends are leaving town
or renovating three-bed semis.
There's the odd
rogue friend
who's eloped with a farmer
and the friend who's making
plotless silent films

but mostly
they're like old dogs to the bushes –
hatching plans
to swarm the suburbs
flee pollution
while I'm still here

polluting farther
not painting a box room
duck egg blue
not tending to watermelons
in South Carolina.

All my friends are leaving town
and have been
for some time.
I suppose
I didn't want to see it

but see it now
as we chase the sun
skim the clouds
bodies losing sight
of time and still

we are still passing
over the Altai.

Love on the Firth

A Scotrail carriage pants into Inverkeithing.
Name unravels along a vacant platform –
bridges black water in heaps of grit, snow, grit, snow.

Granite outcrops like eider nests clarify
to human houses, as the harbour lights blink
beneath a murmuration of domestic planes.

Ecologists say, in a few years, those ducks
could outweigh people. Gulp every rope-grown mussel
before they reach the city's plates.

And that sparse graveyard, those isolate lovers
emerging from the station doors
affirm a slow decline of two-legged bodies:

he in football shorts and a fleece; she in stilettos
and white skinny jeans, hands budding
like crocus shoots around her naked waist

as ice wind asks the shape of love
in the middle of an estuary.

Difficult Children

Mother threads wet plaits through a loom
of fingers: left   right   left   tighten.

From the hotel window we watch as day fades
behind Athena's unplanned mountain –
a mammary rock dropped en route to the citadel
for a spoiled boy in a gilded box.

Mother dropped everything Sunday evenings
to plait my hair in time for school – Medusa curls
so voluminous, I hadn't the heart to ask her
looser, softer. In any case, they grew on me.

Now both of us are turned to gold
from climbing Lycabettus Hill. Tonight
we'll wear almost identical dresses and order
almost identical meals. I'll apply her lipstick
and mascara, in exchange for the master weaving,
and she'll flinch in her sweet, excruciating way.

I know I irritate you sometimes;
I can tell, she says. And I feel the tug
of the plaits, the stone in my chest
without words enough to fix it.

Sleepless in St. Agnes

Beyond the window, Celtic waves crash
like overturned lorries. I throw the duvet off

and writhe in the deep blue stifled room.
It's like the sea is a person trying to warn me

through a mile long tunnel in the cliff face
about a precipice I always expected to meet.

We are too old to be sharing beds with friends.
I know because when one of us capsizes in the dark

bones crack like broken sea glass on the beach.
I know it when my sleepless feet swing down

onto the tiles and carry me outside. Last time
we topped and tailed like this, I was sadder,

you were wilder. There was a different black lab
running with us to the surf and all the time in the world

to drown in it. Now both of you are snoring like soft,
old dogs with little will for walking. But it's 6am.

And yesterday we walked for miles and today we'll walk
for miles and standing here, at the threshold of us,

it seems I've always known the tides would change
once the world was flipped the right way up.

The Marshmallow House

It's an awful lot for one house
to hold, for a house can't wail
about feeling detached
a childhood misspent
the absence of feeling
is nothing of note
for a thing like a house
where I'm watching the words
of the play of my life
like fish in a tank
and I know

I am nowhere near
as attached to my life
as I am to this house –
to all the houses
I have ever known.

Home is a place for boiling water

I

It has stairs to show us ourselves and rooms
for waiting in. Outside there are roses hung
in a state of not quite growing, and beside the door
a last glance mirror sends us up, down.
Nine times out of ten it's easier to stay inside
where peace is a layered flower with a thorny stem.

II

When I belonged there but did not want to
I thought nothing worse than woodchip.
Dandelions trespassed like nosey neighbours
on our driveway and the neighbours, they posed
the same, recycled questions in the same drawl
of middle-england. Everyone was so invested
in a future I wasn't sure I wanted.

III

Every time, before crossing, my mother used to say
there are trolls under that bridge. And every time
I'd be surprised that something so terrible
could live down there, in the unsuspecting stream
flanking swarms of fearless bluebells
so discreetly.

IV

For years I shrunk weekends
reeled in the washing line
from me to there
the years spent mining
restlessly at unhealed skin
the smell of laundry
too long in the drum
as life went on
I couldn't see beyond
the wheezing chimney
thick November nights
as the smoke bellowed
until our faces
were indistinguishable
across the living room.

V

I don't recall the details of the faces in 2008
filing out of the car factory, the chocolate factory;
how every kid got free school meals so stale
we could have thrown them like breeze blocks
through the windscreen of a burning car.

VI

Now that I do not belong there
or speak with the same lilt;
now that I can't say for sure
which kebab shops are old or new;
couldn't tell you who is married, or convicted,
or dead, I want to belong there
more than ever.

Sleep Houses

When you lived in the attic
of the subsiding house
we'd list things alphabetically
until we were too tired to speak.
Now we can afford a warm, dry room –
two rooms – but we've exhausted
British seaside towns and what more
is there to say? I say
we need a new game; I think
the old one only worked
when we were wedged
between ourselves
between the walls
so you tell me
to build a house in my head –
a house like yours or not at all –
a cabin on black sand;
a storm laughing out to sea
waves moved by distant music
unfurled at the legs of your deck chair.
It's easy for you. You already have one
so you just go there, but I would have to start
again – a world I can't, a world I won't
so willingly as you
divulge.

At the centre of my life: my mother dances

after Iyla Kaminsky

By some miracle, every morning
we repeat our role reversal:
she stirs by seven
and the husk of my name drifts
like a blackbird lost
through the cavity wall;
croaks an order of chamomile tea,
codeine, a fromage frais.

Later, when she is happy
and not napping
and not doing a crossword
she'll shed her blanket
to recite a modest sort of dance
with just her hips and hands,
loose trousers swaying,
like a child forgetting
about the cellular mistake
that's grown inside her.

And I feel a swell of guilt
for ever having been a child –
for New Year's Eve two decades ago,
sicker than I'd ever been,
staring at the haze white Christmas tree
I knew she couldn't afford,
with a cold flannel pressed tight

45

to my forehead and changed –
by some miracle –
on the hour.

What have I built?

I suppose it has something to do with the porch
where I opened the trinket shop, selling lumps
of gravel and dandelions through the letterbox

or the cockle shells arranged in a witch's seance
along the edges of our rug, inhaling the smell
of settled soot, door shut. Then something larger:

a damp playhouse under laurel leaves
where I scrawled over the walls in green –
no roads, just trees – and later, two garish bedrooms

in two parents' houses, the car with no door handles,
the dorm room's family of silver fish. As years went by
my architecture became invisible. Things grew from me.

Though lately I've come back to the blueprints.
Assembled chairs for friends who do not visit,
built a porch from matchsticks and a tube of glue
step by step, stick by stick – as if I'd forgotten how already.

Now you ask what I have built and my mouth forms
the shape of nothing. Nothing of consequence.

The face on the field

is not the face it was
a year ago, seven years ago
but there are no folds to say
quite how it changed

> just a woman
> on the other side of the carriage
> doing the same, and I imagine
> I've another five, six,
> until my face on the field
> softens that way

until our eyes meet
in her future reflection
and agree this is
an absurd kind of vanity

> but for now there's a foal
> on my cheek, then no foal,
> and next week I'll be dancing
> even if my shoulders ache
> even if I am tired and ashamed
> of something I barely did
> for the soft, reconciled woman
> I'll be dancing, dancing

Perspective

In a bouillon near Le Sacré-Cœur
I tell my friend for the hundredth time
I wish I could be more like her.
She is never afraid. My friend says –
there are things you're afraid of
and you do them anyway. That
is the definition of brave.

When I get to Mississippi

(if I get to Mississippi)
the roads will be dry, cracked
cambers bending down on either side
into dust.
            Crossing
from Tennessee to Mississippi
the perfect song will play on the radio
after miles of driving with no signal
and the perfect view will slip by
without my noticing.

When I drive through Mississippi
I am always alone

with a stale, empty passenger seat
beside me and a footwell full of books
I'll never read.

            Somewhere
outside Oxford, Mississippi
there's a man in grease-streaked periwinkle
waiting to fill a passing tank, and a woman
out back selling snacks I've never seen
like peanut brittle, moon pies – a man
and a woman and a sky above the pumps
that is taller, sadder
than any sky could ever seem.

            Passing
without a sign, through the bald cypress trees
of Louisiana, I'll trail the hooked vertebrae
of the river – alongside muskrats and cicadas

through the old plantation country
and vow to crawl, some other day,
up one long driveway or another,
fields of cotton either side, trying to decide
if a field can be good and evil
at one time.

Losing love is like a window in your heart.
Words chime as I pass the sign for New Orleans,
where neon streets will be all that I imagined
and all that I imagined will be nothing like
I've ever seen.

I'll stay ('accidentally') on the wrong side of town
and seeing no ounce of desolation
from Katrina – only laughter, only giant vats
of turtle soup stirred behind mesh curtains –
walk towards some neighbours playing music
on a porch. Notes curling upwards
to the same, sad sky and higher

hoping they'll invite me over,
where they've been waiting all this time –
say, *stay, sit a while,* though I do not play
only perch on the splintered deck
beaming.

Lightning Source UK Ltd.
Milton Keynes UK
UKHW010635170722
405957UK00001B/25